BUILDING WITH PROJECT HOME BUILDERS

BUILDING WITH PROJECT HOME BUILDERS

**We trust them to construct our dream homes.
Do our dreams come true?**

Noel Bond

Dedicated to the memory of Margaret Smith Bond:

*There seems no way to repay you for all
you gave us over the years.*

*You gave us guidance and protection —
but also gave us responsibility.*

*You were a shoulder to cry on and a comfort in times
of need — but didn't interfere. You were so many things.
You loved your family unconditionally.*

Dec 10, 1913 - Sept 28, 2006

Copyright © Noel Bond 2017

Building with Project Home Builders written by N.L. Bond. All content written and photographic, is the complete work and property of N.L. Bond. No content or part may be used in any way without the prior written permission of the author. All content is the result of personal experience of the author and no content should be misconstrued as professional advice.

National Library of Australia Cataloguing-in-Publication
Creator: Bond, Noel L., author.
Title: Building with Project Home Builders / Noel L. Bond.
ISBN: 9780995446007 (paperback)

Subjects: House construction.
Architects and builders.
Architecture, Domestic — Designs and plans.
Building — Superintendence.

Typeset in 9/12pt Gotham:
Pickawoowoo Publishing Group
Cover design: Pickawoowoo Publishing Group

Every endeavour has been made to source the photographs and to contact the copyright holders to obtain the necessary permission for use of photographic and quote material used in this book. Any person or organisation that may have been inadvertently overlooked should contact the publisher.

Contents

Introduction	9
The Modern Home	15
Market Research	17
Building a New Home	19
Choosing a Builder	21
Choosing a Floor Plan For Your New Home	25
Changing a Floor Plan Layout	29
Final Working Plan	33
Prestart	35
Going To Site	39
Construction	45
Handover	51
Moving In	53
Some Problems That Could Pop Up	55
Maintenance Period	59
Lowering Standards	63
Making a Claim	65
Not happy with the standard of work performed by the project home builder	67
What liability does a builder have for defective building work under the Home Building Contracts Act	69
Solving Disputes	71
Author Bio	73
Notes	74

Introduction

Was building a new home so stressful, you would never do it again?

We read about them in the press, we hear about them from our friends and family and we experience them ourselves first hand. Good or bad most of us will invest hundreds of thousands of dollars to have them build our dream homes.

Thankfully the majority of us will be totally satisfied with the end result and be willing to recommend the project home builder that built our dream home to others.

Or would we? Personally we would not recommend any project home builder to our friends. At this point it should be said that the information in this book should not be misconstrued as personal building or financial advice but information based on personal experience.

The wife and myself have been dealing with project home builders for a number of years building homes for our own private lifestyle and the life styles of other's, purchasers or renters of the finished project (investment homes).

It has not been unusual for us to have up to five home building projects under way at the same time with five different project home builders on five separate sites finishing one home about every six months.

Why not use one project home builder to build all five homes you may ask; well, no project home builder would build in all five locations that we chose to build in.

In all our experience we would not be able to say we had not encountered potentially stressful situations during construction of any of our homes.

However, we must say that we have not had stressful situations during the construction of all our projects, such projects being in Mandurah Western Australia another in Boyanup Western Australia.

Where the construction and handover of the home progressed reasonably well, at times the landscaping package with the land developer would be drawn out over some six to eight weeks and would take some negotiating just to have a small garden and a little lawn put in at the front of the home.

Point being new home construction may not be at all stressful during the construction stage.

Situations may arise after or before construction and we must remember that by seeing things in their true perspective, what we may see or feel as being an issue may in fact be of little significance to our well being or the completion of the project.

If you find you have a need to get on the phone and complain then be assertive, objective, polite and above all non-abusive.

Most importantly, try not to be reactionary, and give your project home builder the benefit of time to address the item or items you bring to their attention.

There are thousands of people out there managing their own property development portfolios, as we do, though we do not consider ourselves at this point in time to be large property developers.

We do concede that friends knowing of our property developments do see us in this way and are quite interested in our views in choosing and dealing with project home builders.

Also, we get to meet and chat with our fellow neighbours, most of who are also going through the building process.

Neighbours and friends are a very good source of information regarding building experiences and we all love to share our experiences whenever we get an opportunity, it is with our direct experiences and those of people around us that we write.

It is worth mentioning again that we know of no project home builder that we would consider recommending to our friends.

We just feel that if we were to recommend any builder to a friend that their experience would be totally different to our own.

Just as we have experienced project home builders who we have contracted to build two homes at the same time.

We have had two totally different experiences, one project would be going smoothly and the other would need constant attention.

The single most prevalent issue that we have during construction of our homes is time delays.

We have been able to at times use our own tradesmen to do our tiling, painting, paving and grano work at our projects.

This is most helpful when our project home builder is experiencing a shortage of tradespeople to attend our project.

The building supervisors often express their amazement at how fast we are able to get tradespeople on site, when they have huge problems finding tradespeople available to carry out the work.

We are able to get our tradespeople on site fast because we pay them better than project home builders.

If the project home builders performed to a reasonable time schedule, we feel building would not be half as stressful as it seems.

The question would have to be asked, has a project home builder overextended their capabilities by taking on more contracts than they can service, as can happen during building booms.

If there are unreasonable time delays in construction with your project we recommend writing to your builder or contacting your building supervisor and asking for time and date schedules for the completion of your new home in writing.

We can say with our experience the key to a happy and harmonious building experience seems to be in remaining as emotionally detached from the project as possible and getting along amicably with your building supervisor.

It is imperative that you have a good line of communication with your building supervisor, if you are not getting along try to rectify this so the project has a chance to move along nicely and your sanity is maintained.

Building a home for investment seems to be far less stressful than building our personal homes, the only difference being a lack of personal attachment to the investment home.

This is not to mean we don't care as much about the workmanship in our investment homes, we do care with a passion for both our investment and private homes.

We spend two or more hours at our pre-handover inspection irrespective of the purpose of the new home that has been completed.

Somehow we are able to step back and be objective and confident that the builder will make good any little mistakes made along the way.

There is only one way to gain this objective confidence in your project home builder and that is to have a building supervisor handling your project that gives you the confidence in the first place.

Remember this is a two-way street and it is also our responsibility to communicate in a manner that is non-confrontational, keep your building supervisor on your side.

Each time we commence a contract with a project home builder we go through the same process as if it was our first building contract; we are new bees as far as the builder is concerned and we are treated as such.

For this reason we experience a wide range of idiosyncrasies from each builder that can be frustrating, expensive and at times obstructive to a project.

Introduction

It would seem that some project home builders like to employ a policy of admitting to no mistakes and making the customer feel responsible for any little thing that goes wrong in the project.

Although we may have had frustrating experiences with some project home builders, at the end of our projects we have been completely happy with the homes and maintenance done after handover.

It is our intention by sharing our experiences, to help you, the reader overcome some of the little issues that may pop up in the process of building a new home with a project home builder. This book will be helpful in all Australian States and Territories and also New Zealand.

Most importantly, it is our intention to help you understand your relationship with your project home builder. It is also to help you discover the art of communication with the most important people to the success of the construction of your dream home, your initial planning person, prestart person, building supervisor and client liaison person.

Also a project home builder may get some insight into a better understanding of their client's needs, beyond getting a house built and accepting the final payment.

Clients are investing hundreds of thousands of dollars into your ability to build them a home of high standard, but at times, they are let down and made to accept a lower standard that may be more convenient to the project home builder rather than pursuing a satisfactory resolution to an issue.

This has been part of our own personal experience and is how some friends and neighbours have described their experiences with their project home builder.

N. Bond

The Modern Home

Over the past seventeen years we have seen big changes in the homes that are being offered up by the project home builders.

Energy efficiency of homes has been a growing area of achievement.

I believe the efforts taken by project home builders to bring us an energy efficient product over the years has achieved a high standard, so we may enjoy the result of lower energy costs.

We have seen the introduction of solar power in the past seventeen years and recently the introduction of power storage batteries.

It will be very interesting to see how project home builders will package these products into their sales plans in the future.

Home self sufficiency will possibly be the next big target for project home builders to bring to our homes, making for exciting times ahead.

A Wi-Fi home is the norm now; a printer, scanner, fax can be hidden away in a tech cupboard, no need to be taking up desk space in the home office.

In fact, we've done away with the home office in our life; we now use laptops on the alfresco area and a filing cabinet also hidden away.

Home security has come of age with live notifications and recorded video of any movement if you're not at home.

Heat exchange hot water storage systems are an option now, saving more in energy bills.

Outdoor living areas have moved on from pergolas and stuck-on patios to more upmarket alfresco and fully functioning kitchens or barbecues to die for.

Decking has had a makeover from natural timber. We now have a choice of composite decking or natural timber, composite being firmly embraced by us the new home owners.

In the kitchen, we see that hard-to-get-into cupboards are out and large, easy to get to pot draws are definitely in. All drawers and cupboard doors are now soft closing and standard from all good project home builders.

There's a new water supply outlet in the kitchen for refrigerated ice water.

Lighting is all now low energy, including all the nice light fittings you get from your lighting store.

Power outlets can now incorporate USB TV and Internet connections all at one outlet, smart power points are here.

If you're building in an NBN area you can now do away with your land telephone service line and connect it through your service provider to the NBN network.

In the garden the lawn is becoming a smaller area and natural grass is now optional, we are now given a choice of artificial; that is pet and traffic friendly, very low maintenance.

The modern home may still look much the same from the street, but it's on the inside that most of the changes have taken place. The smarter home has evolved over the past seventeen years.

Market Research

The wife calls it market research; I on the other hand call it kidnapping.

It's the process of us going out into new housing estates and seeing first-hand what products look like in new homes.

We could be just going out to find a certain combination of colours and styles in windows, roofs, gutters, bricks, driveways or front doors.

The point of this exercise is to be out there away from the glossy pamphlets, showrooms and display homes seeing how all these materials work in everyday life.

For instance there is a new brick being manufactured that looks excellent in our opinion in a small area as a feature, but we would never consider using this brick as the main house brick.

We had this brick on our short list for a new home, we were about to go to prestart with. We short-listed this brick from the project home builders selection file and the brick manufactures display centre.

Not remembering seeing this brick used anywhere before, Jenny decided it warranted a market research trip out into the new subdivisions to see it in its natural environment.

A new home featuring this new brick was soon found; in fact, more than one was found in a short time and our minds were soon turned away from using it for any of our homes other than in a small feature area.

Now we read about the unfortunate people who did not do their market research and trusted in the sample in the glossy pamphlets or display centre.

Even if they had seen it on a manufacturer's display centre wall, they may not have been able to see the big picture as we did. By seeing a whole home built from these bricks we saw that the home would present unfavourably for our needs.

The project home builder; will assist you to some degree, however, be it on your shoulders if you choose a material or design that turns out to be impractical to your needs, you must do your market research.

Getting a picture of your home in your mind is the first step towards a successful project, irrespective of the project home builder you choose to build with.

Visit the project home builder display centres and familiarise yourself with all materials and designs available.

Building a New Home

- » Is the land suitable for the type of home I want?
- » Does the site have any special engineering requirements?
- » Do the footings and slab require engineering certification?
- » Are there any easements attached to the site?

It is always a very wise move to firstly consider above issues before you commence any building project.

You must consider the soil type and elevation of the land; most importantly, is it sand, limestone or clay soil, is it flat, elevated or sloping land.

Don't assume that you can build a pole home on any slopping land. Ring your local authorities first and ask if there would be any possible objections.

We know of people who have had plans drawn up for a pole home on a nice slopping suburban coastal block to find that the authorities would not permit the construction of a pole home on their site.

Consequently, they were left with the only option; of on selling their slopping coastal block which is still siting as we know not built on by the new owners, maybe with the same problem.

Don't assume that a flat sandy block of land in a coastal subdivision has no limestone under the surface.

Hopefully you won't receive a phone call from your builder telling you they have encountered hard digging on site and that your footings are going to cost more.

We were given two options, dig out the whole site and replace the soil to a certain depth or get a digging machine in to do the digging for the footings.

The digging machine was the cheaper option by far; good thing we followed our golden rule that we work with - budget for the unforseen.

If you adopted this rule throughout your building project you should be able to sleep a little sounder at night knowing that you're not tied to a short shoestring budget.

Your project home builder will advise you on any special requirements for your site. However, be aware at times a special requirement may remain hidden or be overlooked.

An easement may prevent you from building within a certain area on the site; you may have to move your planned home around or change its size to accommodate an easement.

Choosing a Builder

» Is the builder registered? (Ring the Builders' Registration Board in your state to check.)

» Have you checked with the MBA (Master Builders Association) in your state if the builder is a Master Builder?

» Can the builder provide references about homes they have recently completed?

» Is the builder eligible for warranty insurance to cover any defective or incomplete work?

» Have you read and understood the contract?

» Does the contract comply with all the requirements of the Home Building Contracts Act? (The MBA's contract HBW 4 complies)

» Are building permits and planning approvals needed and what is the cost?

Building a new home is one of the biggest investments most people will make in their lives. You need to make sure you make the right decisions at each step along the way.

This avoids costly mistakes, protects the value of your investment and ensures your new home is everything you want it to be.

Avoid making your decisions based primarily on an image that is projected to the public by the project home builder.

We have found that companies with wall-to-wall awards displayed in their offices are not necessarily builders who are focused on our needs as clients.

Cynically, we may conclude that a project home builder with wall-to-wall awards displayed in their office are very good at collecting awards, but may not be equally as good at communicating with you while building your new home.

A good project home builder will work with you at each step along the way assisting you with those right decisions.

Some project home builders unfortunately seem to go out of their way to alienate their clients from a building project.

Having said all this we have had project home builder's who were always pleasant and willing to listen to any questions we asked regarding the progress of our new home.

We have been able to have access to some homes after lock-up simply by going into the project home builder's office and signing out a key and returning it after.

We were able to call in to a particular office any time we were in town and discuss our project face to face over a cup of coffee.

If some were having difficulties getting a tradesperson, tiler or painter they would ask if we knew of one to step in and do the work.

Thankfully, we were able to supply names of tradespeople to our builders.

In the office of most project home builders you will possibly find on a table in the waiting area a file of testimonials from past clients. We advise you to read these if you get the opportunity, you will get some insight into the company you are considering to build your new home.

Remember, if this is your first or tenth building project, be objective and have faith in knowing that project home builders do have a wish to satisfy their clients.

It is in the project home builder's best interest to give good helpful service and to build a quality new home for you.

Also, be comforted in knowing that by using project home builders that meet all the above criteria you have a raft of protection against most mishaps that may arise during and after the construction of your new home.

We have had project home builders close down their offices in the middle of construction of our home, but the project has continued with some frustration but minimal delay.

All warranty insurance to cover defective and incomplete work remains in place; and we maintain our maintenance period. We also maintain our six year structural defects insurance.

If you choose a project home builder that fits the above criteria you will have some protection against the builder closing down in the middle of your project.

Hopefully at the end of your building experience you will be so happy with all that your project home builder has done for you that you will be more than happy to recommend them to other people.

Choosing a Floor Plan For Your New Home

- » Does the design meet your present and future needs?

- » Has provision been made for future additions to the home?

- » Can work be undertaken in stages to suit my budget?

- » Does the design provide for energy efficiency in heating and cooling?

- » What is included in the contract price?

- » Are there variations/extras?

When we begin the process of choosing a floor plan we commence by looking at the site on which we propose to build the home, taking into consideration such things as.

The existing style of other homes in the area, we like to be in keeping with the style of an area as this gives our neighbours and us a better chance of getting along amicably in the long term and preserves investment potential.

With a copy of the dimensions in hand, we stand on the proposed building site and look at all its aspects; front, back and sides.

Can we have a shed here or there, a patio, paving down each side or garden, side gate or drive through garage access to the back yard.

At the front we look at how the home would present to the neighbourhood and in turn how the neighbourhood would present to us, looking out a window in any front room.

Most importantly, we look to see from which way the weather comes and its effects on how and where we place rooms, entries and exits in the proposed home.

Try not to have too much wet weather blowing into areas such as front entry, side laundry or outdoor entertaining areas.

Also remember that potential excessive heat may not be desirable in some areas, so we need to be mindful of finding a balance.

So with some idea of the dimensions, aspects and outlooks of the block of land we are intending to build on we are able to go shopping for a preliminary floor plan from a project home builder.

We tend to choose our preliminary floor plans from display home centres. We do this because we get a good feel for what the trends are doing in the way of colours, materials, and landscaping plus all over designs.

New home sections in the weekend newspapers are also a good source for preliminary floor plans.

We may go to three or four display home centres and look at each project home builder's floor plans, shortlisting any we feel may suit our needs.

The project home builder's rep (the fellow sitting at the dining table) will be happy to chat with you and guide you in your quest to find a suitable floor plan for your needs. If not go to the display home next door and seek information from the rep there.

After looking at ten to twenty display homes and collecting floor plans all afternoon you would probably be understandably confused but hopefully excited at the prospect of knowing that you may have in your possession a floor plan that will suit your needs.

At home, we come to a decision as to what plan we are going with, a plan that we can bend and tweak to suit our needs with little effort and with the assistance of the project home builder's rep (the fellow that was sitting at the dining table) at the display home.

We know we should have no problems adding or subtracting doors and windows and so forth with his assistance.

You may choose to enquire about using the floor plan of the display home that you have come to, with a view of maybe making some minor adjustments.

After all, you can see the finished home and there is no need to imagine too much, as some people dislike interpreting floor plans.

Bear in mind and the project home builder's rep will inform you of this, that some room sizes in the display home may be larger than the standard for that home.

Also, some fittings will not be standard, such as some tap fittings, floor tiles, blinds, overhead cupboards and painting walls may very well be extra cost.

Be aware of the size of the garage, we have often found that the depth of garages to be barely adequate when it comes to garaging a family vehicle.

You should ask the question what comes as standard with this home if I, we were to contract your company to build it.

We have used the floor plans of display homes at times and we are mindful as we walk through, that not all we see, may be standard to the floor plan or fittings.

Building a home for our own lifestyle from a display centre, we added sixty thousand dollars, to the cost of constructing the display home.

We made changes such as higher quality fittings; better floor plan layout, making the home larger and higher with coffered ceilings and adding a three-vehicle garage and so on.

The point being, your budget and your lifestyle will dictate to you the extent of changes if any, you will make to the home you build.

We have found that we usually contract to build with the company, whose rep has been the most pleasant, helpful and obliging in the first instance.

The person at the display home (project home builder's representative) is without a doubt the most influential person in the whole process of you building your dream home with this company.

Therefore, you should both be happy to work together.

Changing a Floor Plan Layout

Any structural changes that use additional material or labour will incur additional costs to you.

All project home builders will allow you to make changes to their plan to enable you to personalise the finished home to your needs (each builder has a cut off point, some allow only two or three changes others more).

If the plan you choose from any builder fits all your needs (lifestyle and budget) then go with it, the less changes you make to the plan the less complicated and less stressful the whole project will be for you and the project home builder.

We tend to leave a floor plan basically as we find it, if we're building for on sale or a home for rental purposes.

All our homes have a dishwasher recess, doors to all robes, upgrade standard doors to stanford doors, outdoor gas outlet, and an attractive front elevation.

Remember, it is in the best interest of any project home builder for you to have a pleasant building experience with them, therefore they like you to work with their basic plan as close as possible. (Minimal changes, minimal confusion and minimal stress.)

Most changes will incur a cost if you wish to have a door on a robe where on the plan there is no door. You will need to know that the cost of the door frame, door, door knob and painting will be calculated and added to your costs.

If you see that you will need to have more power points in any room the cost will be calculated and added to your cost's. (Discuss power points at your prestart meeting.)

You may need to make the home or a room larger. In this case, simply adding an extra metre down the middle, or building out into the eave space may accomplish this, at an extra cost to you.

All additional costs or credits (variations) as a result of your changes to the plan will be itemised for you to see and sign off on, at prestart meeting.

Any deleted doors, windows, internal walls and so on, should result in a credit back to you and it's up to you to be on your toes and remind them that you have a credit if this is the case. Or use this credit elsewhere in the home.

Thankfully, there are quite a lot of changes you can make to a plan and incur no or very little cost.

You may flip a plan at no additional cost left or right, you may relocate items such as light switches, power point's, lights, some walls, doors, windows and you may move rooms around at no additional cost in some cases; if you're still working in the original plan area.

Some builders will allow you to add windows at no extra cost as they see a window as being the same cost as supplying and laying bricks in a cavity wall.

We commonly relocate our laundry taps and cabinet in the garage and add 600mm in width to the garage giving us more room to accommodate a full laundry in the garage and more room in the house for much larger bedrooms and bathrooms.

We also relocate the laundry sliding door to a bedroom and add on a nice timber deck courtyard after construction. The extra cost is only the cost of adding 600mm or so in width to the garage and the cost of adding an exit door in the garage to the clothes line.

Dishwasher recess should be a freebie, flyscreens to all windows, Colorbond or tile roof may be a free choice and driveway crossover costs should be included in a standard building contract. Some builders charge extra so we avoid them.

If the building industry is slowing down after a building boom in your area you should see builders starting to discount items and adding free incentives like ducted air conditioning to all rooms. Take advantage of all that you're given, you're paying in the long run so you may as well have it.

Final Working Plan

After your preliminary plan is complete and you're happy with the location of everything, your new dream home will be ready to go to planning for preparation of final working plans.

This is where all your changes are formally drawn up as a final working plan representing the home you will contract the project home builder to build for you, and this is where you make your first payment towards your new dream home, usually around one thousand dollars. (Usually non-refundable.)

Builders differ at most stages and there is no exception at this stage. Your plans will be drawn up and posted out to you in three to six weeks depending on your builder.

Ask the person who assisted you with transforming your basic preliminary plan into a final working plan, how long the proses will take. They will be happy to give you some idea of the time frame.

You may not be dealing with this person from here on. After your preliminary plan goes off to planning you may not see it again until it is posted to you as your final working plan.

When you receive your final working plans in the post be sure to go over all details carefully looking at the position of the house on the block of land, lot number, street name, all elevations, floor plan, electrical plan (power points and light placement at prestart).

Pay attention to any changes you made from the basic preliminary plan to the final working plans. If something is wrong, let them know ASAP or at your prestart meeting.

Also, you will receive in the post a folder crammed full of all your selection options in styles and colours for your, bricks, roofing, paving, windows, taps, shower heads, painting colours, kitchen sink, oven, cooktop and so on.

You will also be given an opportunity to select from your project home builder's basic range at the prestart meeting.

Note: not all the styles or materials, in the folder may be available to you for whatever reason, so it's often wise to be prepared to change something in your selection at the prestart meeting.

You should also be informed as to which ceramic tile store; you are to go to. To make your selection of internal tiles, bench tops and cupboard doors from the brand names of your selection range.

You will need to make all your bathroom, kitchen and laundry, tile selections and bench top selections before you go to your prestart meeting.

The paper work compiled at the tile shop will catch up with you again at the prestart meeting.

Note: your contract may not include tiling to the laundry and WC floor; make inquires now at the planning stage and include tiling to the laundry and WC floor in your budget.

Prestart

You will be notified by mail by the project home builder that they are ready for you to make an appointment with them for the prestart meeting.

We have mentioned that you will need to have seen your final working plans and made your selections at the tile shop.

You will have given all consideration to all your colour selections, both inside and out, bricks, windows, roof material and colour before your prestart meeting.

Also, it may be beneficial to consider three-phase or single-phase power and the inclusion of smart power metering at this stage.

It's also recommended that you have a good knowledge (copy) of your additional costs or credits (variations) that you signed off on; at this meeting you will be referring to it again.

If you sit down at the prestart meeting without a clue, you may be in for a long day or two while the prestart person takes you over every inch of your home trying to get this information out of you.

We have managed to complete a prestart meeting in one hour, but we have had the eight-hour meeting, mainly because of a lack of communication and failure of planning to get things correct on the final working plan.

Also at that meeting we had a prestart person trying to ride over us in our choice of paint colour and what brand name we could use and what roofing material we could use.

The home we were building was advertised with a choice of metal roof or tiled roof at no extra charge, we chose metal at the planning stage no problems. On the plan, we noticed a tile roof was specified not metal.

We mentioned this at the prestart meeting and suddenly we were going to be charged to have a metal roof. We produced the full advertisement from the newspaper and we were told it was possibly a misprint.

We were given the roof we had chosen, after some haggling and were able to use any paint colour of our choice, regardless of brand name.

There is no reason for your prestart meeting to be stressful, so long as you're going in prepared to make some minor adjustments.

Maybe you overlooked something, such as choosing an ornate border tile in your tile selection, or not being aware that your builder and most builders are going to charge you extra to have them laid.

This could certainly cause some stress if you had set your heart on the ornate border tile, and suddenly you are faced with having to choose, pay more or give the ornate border tile up.

At times such as this having a little flexibility in your budget will be most helpful.

As a rule of thumb the more you work outside your budget and the box the builder would like you to work in, the more likely you are to feel you're being faced with increased costs.

At the prestart meeting you will be asked to sign off on the construction of your new home.

Supposing all has gone well at your meeting and all signing off has been completed to the satisfaction of all, your dream home will now go to site.

You should be given the name and phone numbers of your building supervisor and your client liaison person in the office to contact throughout the building of your home.

Note: The building supervisor and your client liaison person will now be the most important and influential people in the success of the completion of your new home.

Ask how long the construction time will take from this day; in a building boom expect construction to take in excess of twelve months and in quiet times expect no less than six months.

Appreciate that your building supervisor will possibly have twenty or more other homes under their control - most have an ability to make you feel you are the only client.

Give your building supervisor space, time and some understanding and they will construct your home with little inconvenience to you.

Going To Site

- » Preparation of the Building Site
- » Under slab plumbing and footings
- » Concrete house slab
- » Delivery of bricks or framing
- » Delivery of building materials, window frames, door frames, mortar, sand and shed
- » Commencement of bricklaying or framing, (to plate height)
- » Delivery of roofing material, timber or steel trusses
- » Roof pitch
- » Delivery of roofing tiles or metal sheeting and fixing to pitched roof
- » Gutters, downpipes and ventilation flumes
- » Electrical wiring
- » External and Internal plumbing placement
- » Internal hard wall plastering or dry wall fixing to stud or brick walls
- » Installing glass to windows and doors to entries
- » Installing ceilings

- Lock-up
- Installing vanities, kitchen cupboards, robes shelving, internal doors
- Tiling to wet areas and kitchen
- Approach builders tiler to quote on tiling to living areas and laundry (if applicable)
- Fitting of internal tapware, hot water service, fitting of power points, light sockets, wall oven, hot plates, rangehoods and exhaust fans
- Painting of ceilings, doors, frames and all external fittings gutters, downpipes and eaves
- Approach builder's painter to quote on painting internal walls (if applicable)
- Pavers or concrete in the garage, alfresco and driveway
- Installing insulation to roof space
- Fitting of flyscreens
- Clean house, windows, window tracks, bench tops, sinks, inside cupboards, floors and so forth
- Removal of all site rubbish and site levelled
- Handover
- Maintenance period

You can choose to drive past your building site each day, but remember a watched kettle never boils.

At this point we would like to mention that if you feel the task of monitoring your building project is way beyond your ability, we recommend you consider appointing your own independent building inspector.

You employ your independent building inspector to monitor your project; who will report to you or your building supervisor any defective workmanship.

The builder should have a policy to phone you, (progress report) as certain stages of construction are about to commence, and for some people this may be sufficient.

We keep a much closer relationship going with our building supervisors; we monitor the whole construction of our homes and inform the project home builders of any major issues, if they happen.

This is not to say that we would not consider appointing our own independent building inspector in any future projects; on the contrary this would be most advantageous to our needs.

It would not be beneficial to be overly critical of workmanship or mistakes that are of a minor nature, give your builder the benefit of your trust in their ability to get things done and put things right.

In some instances we have not met or had needed to speak to our building supervisor until the project is at handover.

On the other hand, we have been at site meetings and on the phone nonstop with others.

If the building is coming along smoothly, we are quite happy to just monitor the project, but we will not hesitate in making contact if needed.

Your building supervisor will be happy to meet you on site to take you through your home at any stage of the construction we recommend you take full advantage of all your on-site inspections with your building supervisor.

We have found that the progress reports we get from some project home builders are very much out of sync with what is actually happening at the construction site.

For instance, we have received progress reports to inform us that the house slab is about to be put down in a week or so, two weeks after we ourselves have observed it being put down.

We have been informed that bricks are about to arrive on site days after their arrival on site.

Also, we have received progress reports for other people's homes that are misleading and quite embarrassing for the person phoning, suppose we must allow for some small mistakes and remain optimistic about the project home builders capabilities.

In some states it may not be possible to go onto a building site because the site is fenced with security fencing.

This is a very necessary precaution to prevent the entry of thieves and vandals; there is nothing more frustrating than having good work ruined and time delays caused by foolish theft or vandalism.

Subject to safety requirements the builder in most states must permit you, the owner (or a person authorised by the owner) to have reasonable access to the building site and to view any part of the building work.

However, any person who is granted this access must not interfere with the carrying out of the works and if they should do so the builder may be entitled to extra costs for any delay or interference caused.

If you happen to see something strange on your building site report it to your building supervisor and help your builder fight crime at vacant building sites by noting down licence numbers and times of day of unusual happenings.

Also keep an eye out for other building teams working for other project home builders, if a home is being built on an adjoining property to yours.

We have actually unplugged the power and disconnected water, where the tradesperson working there was using our supply to service an adjoining property.

When we get water bills in excess of five hundred dollars for a building project we take exception at supplying water or power to other people's new homes.

Construction

Site works will involve the preparation of the building site, removal of or adding to topsoil, levelling the site and compaction of the house pad area.

It will also include preparation for laying of footings, placement of under slab plumbing and the installation of temporary water and power supplies.

The concrete house slab can be very deceiving in its overall size, and imagining where all the rooms are going to fit in such a small space can be difficult.

Have faith, the overall area of your slab will accommodate all the rooms of your new home.

When the bricks are delivered on site just check that the correct style and colour have been delivered.

Internal bricks will most likely be placed on the slab and the external bricks will be placed around the slab.

Door and window frames will have been delivered to site, a portable shed for storage of mortar and small items, a load of clean sand on site and construction to plate height is about to commence.

During the bricklaying be considerate and keep out of the way of the bricklaying team as it is not advisable to get under any tradesperson's feet while they are working.

Most tradespeople are quite happy to give some explanation as to how and why they do things this way or that but remember they are the professionals.

If you have an issue with the standard of work or something not going as per plan, consult with your building supervisor and let them know of your concerns.

Something we find comes up time and again at the bricking stage is the lack of ties used to tie in sliding patio or laundry doors to the brickwork.

It becomes apparent that insufficient tying in has occurred when the sliding door frame is loose, when opening or closing the door.

Assuming your bricking team is top notch all the brickwork should be completed to top plate height in two to three weeks and roofing timber will soon be on site to commence the pitch of the roof.

Roof pitching can be done in timber or preformed steel trusses or not preformed.

Whichever choice you're given by your builder the end result should be satisfactory with no sagging over time.

Whether you have chosen tiles or metal sheeting as your roof covering, you are hoping for a weatherproof finish, we must say we have had no problems using metal roof sheeting as opposed to tiles. (It's a personal choice)

Be prepared to tell the building supervisor that there are leaks if you use tiles.

The covering of a standard roof usually takes one to four days in good weather.

Gutters, downpipes and ventilation flumes should follow closely along with the electrical wiring of the home and installation of plumbing in the roof space and walls.

Internal hard wall plastering or dry wall fixing to stud or brick walls will commence next, some builders are now offering dry wall to internal brick walls in place of hard wall plaster.

Some would prefer this option, as it must eliminate cracking of walls as seen in some cases in hard wall plaster walls.

However, if the brick laying and the hard wall plastering is of good quality surely there should be no cracking of walls seen. (It's a personal choice)

You may notice that some power point and light switch wiring has been covered over, don't panic they will be located again.

All the sheeting for the ceilings (Gyprock) will appear on site, placed under cover together with lengths of cornice.

The ceilings and cornice will be professionally installed in a week or two, depending on the size and difficulty of the work to be done.

Congratulations, your building supervisor should now be in a position to be able to lock your home, having installed window glass and fitted external doors.

You will now have to peer through windows to see what happenings are going on at your home, if before you were able to walk through your home.

If like us you like to be a sticky beak and you do peer through the windows after lock-up, you may find that a trades person has inadvertently left a door or window open.

We often find this to be the case; we take a look around inside the home and lock-up when leaving.

If you have arranged with your builder that you will be supplying some light fittings, internal or external, now would be an advantageous time to supply them for installation.

We often supply our own light fittings for the builder's electrician to install for us at an additional cost; we have also supplied our own range hoods in some cases.

You must have your fittings available on time for installation, or suffer the consequences of not having them installed.

There will be trades people at your home almost each day now, if your building supervisor is doing their work diligently.

You should see:

» Installing of bathroom vanities, kitchen cupboards, robes shelving, and internal doors

» Tiling to wet areas bathroom, laundry and kitchen splash backs

- » Fitting of internal tapwear and hot water service

- » Fitting of power points, light sockets, wall oven, hot plates, rangehoods and exhaust fans

- » Painting of ceilings, doors, frames and all external fittings gutters and downpipes

- » Laying of pavers or pouring of concrete in the garage, alfresco and driveway

- » Site cleanup, which will involve a bobcat, scooping up all lose building material (rubbish) on the site and leveling of your building site

If this work is not being done in good time six to eight weeks, then ask your supervisor what is the hold up.

It's not unusual that work comes to a standstill for weeks for no apparent reason with most project home builders.

If this is the case with your home then phone your supervisor to ask questions as to why there is a standstill at your property.

We have found amongst project home builders that it has been a common practice to assign unrealistic numbers of new homes to their supervisors.

We have had a supervisor with fifty new homes assigned to him and because of this our project was suffering long delays.

Tradespeople were not being booked to do the smallest of jobs because they were being overlooked.

It was very clear to us that this company was focused only on volume; hopefully your project home builder will be outcome and client focused.

While you have your supervisor's attention at this point in time you should be able to get a firm commitment to a completion time of your home your supervisor will be happy to give you a completion and handover date.

Handover

Supposing you're given a completion and handover date, what should you expect on this date?

You will meet with your building supervisor at your new home, who will walk through the home with you room by room.

Take this opportunity to open and close each door, window, cabinet, draws, and cupboards; run taps, flush toilets, operate hotplates, oven and exhaust fans.

Take a note pad with you and note down any things you feel are out of place, discus your findings with your supervisor.

The supervisor and yourself will conduct a walk around the outside of your home; follow the same principle.

We have had good and bad supervisors; one who would not give us his phone number and only met with us on handover day, and one who was actually able and willing to point out things that needed attention before the home was handed over to us.

Take notes, discuss your findings with your supervisor.

Pay attention to the site clean up, has all rubbish been removed and is the site level again as before the commencement of construction.

If your home is completed, 100 per cent to your satisfaction sign off on the completion of your new home and receive your keys and hamper from your supervisor. (Your new home is yours)

As we stated in our introduction, at the end of our projects we have been completely happy with the homes and maintenance done after handover.

However, we have had issues that have stalled the handover of the home.

If we come across such an issue, it stalls handover in that we simply do not sign off on the completion of the project, we do not take possession of any keys until the issue has been attended to.

This may be feasible if you're not intending to move into your new home straightaway, however, not too many people are in that position.

You may have been paying rent during the construction of your new home plus the interest payments on the new home.

If the home you have just completed is an investment property you may be paying your interest on your loan and need to get your tenant into your property ASAP to offset your costs.

So the best way to deal with any minor problems you may find with the finish of your new home at handover is to make a list of faults that you feel should be fixed by your project home builder. (Maintenance List)

Your supervisor will be happy to discuss your concerns and get the problem fixed in the most convenient way for you.

Moving In

A checklist of things to remember to do:

- » Notify power, gas and telephone
- » Insurance – home, contents and medical
- » Newspaper delivery
- » Milk delivery
- » Children's schools and clubs
- » Banks and credit accounts
- » Associations and memberships
- » Subscriptions
- » Collect new bus, train timetables
- » Vehicle and drivers licensing
- » Your employer
- » Redirection of your mail
- » Farewell to neighbours
- » Housewarming date and invitations

Some Problems That Could Pop Up

- » Sliding patio or laundry doors not adequately tied into brickwork
- » Gaps between eaves lining and brickwork
- » Site clean up and levelling at completion not adequate
- » Internal house clean at completion not adequate
- » Downpipes and external plumbing not secured to brickwork
- » Guttering not straight or fitting loosely
- » Large chips on rendered corners, or edges of rendered window sills
- » Shower floor not draining away
- » Scratches to bench tops or paint work
- » Kitchen bench tops or sink not secured down
- » Cracked ceramic tile
- » Broken window glass
- » Water pipe leaking
- » Water hammer in plumbing

- Sand in plumbing lines
- Door opening wrong way
- Door not opening or closing smoothly
- Door striker plate missing
- Drill holes in internal or external brickwork
- Roof tile or tiles not in place
- Painting not satisfactorily completed
- Over-spray on internal walls, where doors were painted
- Over-spray on windows
- Internal walls not left white
- Damaged flyscreens
- Brick Paving or grano work not satisfactory
- Loose fittings
- Cracks in walls, internal or external
- External brick cleaning not satisfactory, allow mineral seepage
- Power point or light switches lose or missing covers
- Telephone or TV points missing
- Scuff marks around manhole covers

Some Problems That Could Pop Up

- » Marks on ceiling or walls, allow mineral seepage to hard walls
- » Sink drain or floor waste covers not fitted
- » Damage to existing fencing, structures
- » Large gaps around window frames internal or external

Be observant; don't overlook the little things when inspecting your new home for the first time. Allow a minimum of two hours with your supervisor on site.

Rest assured that if you were to find any one of the problems above in your new home, your project home builder (building supervisor) would definitely rectify them before or after handover.

Maintenance Period:

The maintenance period commences after handover of your new home and depending on your builder runs for three to four months after handover.

Some builders may offer you a cash payout in lieu of them coming back to do any maintenance. This payment may be around two hundred and fifty dollars or above.

During the maintenance period your project home builder may fix any problems you found in the handover. (Maintenance list)

In addition to any problems you picked up, then your builder will at the end of the three to six month maintenance period fix any other problems you find in relation to the construction of your new home.

Also, any problems that are fixed may also qualify for a further three to six months maintenance period after attention.

We assume your project home builder has allowed for the cost of this maintenance period when costing your project way back at the beginning. We recommend you use it.

Getting the project home builder back to do the maintenance does tend to pose a problem. We have experienced long delays of over twelve months in getting our maintenance completed with a particular builder.

In fact, we could have been forgiven for feeling forgotten if not for the fact that we regularly contacted them to be sure we had not been forgotten.

We hear from our friends that getting maintenance done has been drawn out and difficult to arrange with their project home builders also.

This is far from satisfactory for any project home builder and certainly does not put their name in good stead when people get together with friends and discuss their project home building experiences.

We should also mention that we have had the experience where we required no maintenance at all after handover during the maintenance period.

This was an exception as it was the only home out of the five we had built at that time. We did not sign off on the completion until we were happy all work was completed.

We had a good building supervisor who focused on customer satisfaction and presenting a finished product.

We were able to have this property on the market for sale the same day we signed off and received the keys.

The supervisor was aware that we intended to have the home on the market and was quite prepared to have the home 100 per cent ready for us at handover.

So try not to have a huge list of little fix ups post handover pasted onto your maintenance period.

Use this period to fix any other problems you find in relation to the construction of your new home after you take possession.

Cracks in external brickwork.

Gaps around window frames.

Render not satisfactory.

Sliding door not tied into brickwork.

Paint spatter on brick work.

Mortar pointing not complete.

Site made clean and level.

Stand back to see roof line.

Check paving pattern is correct.

Site prepared for concrete slab.

Operate all appliances and tapware.

Roof frame may be timber or metal.

Private tradespeople are most helpful.

Fencing on building sites prevents injury.

All fittings are fastened in place.

Mineral seepage is not a concern.

Little things often overlooked.

A happy home and a smooth project.

Water damage after living in a home.

Ready for landscaping.

Lowering Standards

Something we have observed over the time we have been involved with project home builders is their apparent willingness to embrace a lower standard.

Australia's building codes and standards come under review often and in this process standards invariably change.

The outcome should be of a higher standard we like to imagine, but this is not necessarily the case.

If you notice that something does not look to be of a high standard, maybe it is within the standard.

We have in the past noticed that after two coats of a light coloured paint on guttering, we have been able to see metal streaks under the paint.

The builder may have applied the paint as specified, undercoat plus two coats of paint, within Australia's building codes and standards.

However, because the colour was light (surf mist) a little more attention to coverage may have been required.

A third coat was applied and we were happy; however, was the builder obliged to do so? Maybe not, after all it was only our sharp eye that spotted it in the first place.

We all find ourselves at some time asking how did they get away with that?

The answer is that it very possibly meets Australia's building codes and standards.

They don't make them like they used to, but we most certainly have the right to question the standard of any work or finish to our homes.

If we all continually accept a lower finish, that finish may soon become the standard, this may equally apply to any service provider and client situation.

Good luck with your project.

Making a Claim

If after living in your new home for two or three years you experience a plumbing leak you should consider.

- » Turning off your mains water
- » Calling a private plumber
- » Calling your project home builders plumber
- » Notifying your home insurer
- » Notifying your project home builders of a structural fault claim

We have had this experience after living in a home for 18 months, so we are able to share with you the process of getting it fixed.

If your leak is the result of an accident, storm, wind or rain, then read your home insurance policy and phone your insurer for more details and further instruction.

Our home insurance policy clearly stated that we were not covered for damage caused as a result of building defects or faulty workmanship.

We phoned our project home builder's plumber after reading our project home builder's insurance policy and they were most helpful in getting out to us to see what the problem was.

The plumber arrived and we showed him where the water was leaking in the laundry ceiling and he proceeded to fix the problem.

In approximately ten minutes he found a very small split in the PVC water pipe in the ceiling space and replaced a section of pipe.

We were able to call on our builder because we have six years of protection against defects such as materials and workmanship.

We were also able to arrange for the project home builder's maintenance team to come and repaint the ceiling and wall where the water stained the paintwork.

The latter part of the process may take considerable time because the project home builder will see paintwork repairs as being low priority and their maintenance team will be very hard pushed to get to your job considering they possibly have two to three hundred new homes to maintain.

Maybe if the paintwork repairs are very minor it may be worth considering doing the work yourself.

Not happy with the standard of work performed by the project home builder

Many disputes between owners and project home builders can be very quickly resolved through good communication and discussions. You should contact the project home builder and raise any concerns and discuss them with the builder.

Generally the matter will be resolved. If you the owner are not happy with the outcome, dispute-settling procedures are set out in your contract document.

You may wish to consider seeking independent legal advice (for a referral to a qualified solicitor phone the Law Society) or appoint a private inspector to provide a written report or, as a last resort, lodge a claim with the Building Disputes Tribunal in your state.

It should always be remembered, however, that to run a dispute costs money and time. It is always best for the project home builder and owner to try and settle all disputes between themselves first and not resort to other measures such as legal proceedings. Remember, you both have to work together as a team under your building contract for your project to be a success and an enjoyable experience.

What liability does a builder have for defective building work under the Home Building Contracts Act

The builder is required to repair any defects that appear within three to four months of practical completion. This is known as the defects liability period, or maintenance period. Complaints that building has not been done in a proper and workmanlike manner, including complaints of structural defects, can be made under the Builders' Registration Act for up to six years after practical completion. This is so, regardless of whether the property changes hands over the period.

Solving Disputes

If a dispute arises, you may wish to take some or all of the following steps:

- » Discuss the matter with your builder or building supervisor
- » Advise the builder in writing if the problem is still not resolved
- » Seek a private building inspection for independent advice
- » Contact the Building Disputes Tribunal in your state to register your dispute
- » Seek a hearing before a private arbitrator or before the Building Disputes Tribunal in your state

Anyone who has engaged a builder/contractor to do building work can approach the tribunal to settle an outstanding dispute, as long as:

The dispute is about unsatisfactory work (where the contract is in excess of six thousand dollars); or it is a contractual dispute (where the contract is for home building work valued between six thousand dollars and two hundred thousand dollars).

The Building Disputes Tribunal has the power to adjudicate on disagreements between owners and builders. It can issue several types of orders against a builder whose work is found to be unsatisfactory. These orders may require the builder to undertake additional work, rectify unsatisfactory work or may require the builder to pay the owner a sum of money.

NCAT. NSW Civil and Administrative Tribunal: www.ncat.nsw.gov.au/

SAT W.A. www.sat.justice.wa.gov.au/B/building_disputes.aspx

W.A. *Building Services (Complaint Resolution and Administration) Act 2011:* www.commerce.wa.gov.au/building-commission/building-service-and-home-building-work-contract-complaints

QCAT. Queensland: http://www.qcat.qld.gov.au/matter-types/building-disputes

VCAT. Victorian Civil and Administrative Tribunal: www.vcat.vic.gov.au

CBS. South Australia: www.cbs.sa.gov.au

Resolving Building Disputes Department of Justice Tasmania: www.justice.tas.gov.au/building/disputes

Northern Territory Building Complaints and Disputes: nt.gov.au/property/building-and-development/building-complaints-and-disputes/?SQ_PAINT_LAYOUT_NAME=multi-parent&curr=203607&print=yes

ACAT. Australian Capital Territory: www.acat.act.gov.au/

BDT. New Zealand: www.buildingdisputestribunal.co.nz/

Author Bio

My grandfather was a carpenter, builder who emigrated from London, England to Western Australia in the late 1800s. In 1986-87 I constructed my first home a four-by-two double brick home. This was a very long but very rewarding undertaking being an owner-builder, but something I would not undertake again. There must be something to the DNA memory theory because I do get satisfaction from construction of homes with project home builders. Maybe as my grandfather got satisfaction from his building projects I have this desire to fulfil through project home builders.

Notes

www.ingramcontent.com/pod-product-compliance
Lightning Source LLC
Chambersburg PA
CBHW070550300426
44113CB00011B/1856